HEY YOU !

YOU KNOW ALL THOSE THINGS YOU'VE ALWAYS WANTED TO DO ?

YOU SHOULD DO THEM !

NOTES

5 GREAT BIG

HUGS

FOR 2017

Because EVERYONE loves a
BIG HUG!

Huge Unbelievable Goals

Write down 5 of your biggest goals for 2017 – You know, so big you might not know how to make them happen, but not so big they are completely unachievable. They could be business or personal. They should also be OUTCOME based and not ACTIVITY based. They should be a little bit scary but ever so exciting ☺

Most of all they should be FUN - FUN - FUN

HUG – Goal	WHY is it important?
[Example] To increase my revenue by at least 20%	To make sure my business continues to grow.
1.	
2.	
3.	
4.	
5.	

Draw a picture, write a big number or cut
out an image that represents my HUG's

HUG #1

HUG #2

HUG #3

Have some fun with
finding ways to represent
my BIG HUGS

I must do this bit!!!
Ian says they add more
value than I think

HUG #4

HUG #5

SOME BASIC INFO. ABOUT MY BUSINESS

Knowing the numbers in my business is VITAL to my SUCCESS

[Coaches Tip] If you don't know any of these numbers then sit down with your accountant or bookkeeper and ask them to help you. They will help you to set some great goals and objectives for 2017.

It's pointless trying to improve something if you can't measure it.

These are my numbers from last year

My Turnover for 2015-16 How much I generated in sales last year	
My NET Profit for 2015-16 How much I made last year after all my fixed and variable costs are deducted.	
My Breakeven The amount I need to run my business & before I make a profit.	
My Conversion rate (As a percentage) How many leads I need to see before I make a sale represented as a percentage	
My NET Profit Margin (As a percentage) How much money I made after fixed and variable costs are subtracted.	
My repeat business as an average How often my customers come back to me and give me repeat business as an average.	
My Average order value The average order value for all my sales. Total sales value divided by the number of sales.	

7 STEPS TO SUCCESS:

1 MAKE A COMMITMENT TO GROW DAILY

2 VALUE THE PROCESS MORE THAN EVENTS

3 DON'T WAIT FOR INSPIRATION

4 BE WILLING TO SACRIFICE PLEASURE FOR OPPORTUNITY

5 DREAM BIG

6 PLAN YOUR PRIORITIES

7 GIVE UP TO GO UP

SO FAR...

My biggest SUCCESSES

My biggest CHALLENGES

DON'T LOOK BACK

YOU'RE NOT GOING THAT WAY

YOU NEVER KNOW HOW CLOSE YOU ARE...
NEVER GIVE UP ON YOUR DREAMS!

2017 EVENTS

Important key events (by month) that will be important to me in 2017

January	February	March

April	May	June

July	August	September

October	November	December

SOMETIMES YOU WIN

SOMETIMES YOU LEARN

SWOT!!!

What are my personal STRENGTHS, WEAKNESSES, OPPORTUNITIES & THREATS?

S

W

O

T

January	February	March	April	May	June
1 Su New Year's Day	1 We	1 We	1 Sa	1 Mo Early May Bank Hol. 18	1 Th
2 Mo Substitute day 1	2 Th	2 Th	2 Su	2 Tu	2 Fr
3 Tu	3 Fr	3 Fr	3 Mo 14	3 We	3 Sa
4 We	4 Sa	4 Sa	4 Tu	4 Th	4 Su
5 Th	5 Su	5 Su	5 We	5 Fr	5 Mo 23
6 Fr	6 Mo 6	6 Mo 10	6 Th	6 Sa	6 Tu
7 Sa	7 Tu	7 Tu	7 Fr	7 Su	7 We
8 Su	8 We	8 We	8 Sa	8 Mo 19	8 Th
9 Mo 2	9 Th	9 Th	9 Su	9 Tu	9 Fr
10 Tu	10 Fr	10 Fr	10 Mo 15	10 We	10 Sa
11 We	11 Sa	11 Sa	11 Tu	11 Th	11 Su
12 Th	12 Su	12 Su	12 We	12 Fr	12 Mo 24
13 Fr	13 Mo 7	13 Mo 11	13 Th	13 Sa	13 Tu
14 Sa	14 Tu	14 Tu	14 Fr Good Friday	14 Su	14 We
15 Su	15 We	15 We	15 Sa	15 Mo 20	15 Th
16 Mo 3	16 Th	16 Th	16 Su	16 Tu	16 Fr
17 Tu	17 Fr	17 Fr	17 Mo Easter Monday 16	17 We	17 Sa
18 We	18 Sa	18 Sa	18 Tu	18 Th	18 Su
19 Th	19 Su	19 Su	19 We	19 Fr	19 Mo 25
20 Fr	20 Mo 8	20 Mo 12	20 Th	20 Sa	20 Tu
21 Sa	21 Tu	21 Tu	21 Fr	21 Su	21 We
22 Su	22 We	22 We	22 Sa	22 Mo 21	22 Th
23 Mo 4	23 Th	23 Th	23 Su	23 Tu	23 Fr
24 Tu	24 Fr	24 Fr	24 Mo 17	24 We	24 Sa
25 We	25 Sa	25 Sa	25 Tu	25 Th	25 Su
26 Th	26 Su	26 Su	26 We	26 Fr	26 Mo 26
27 Fr	27 Mo 9	27 Mo 13	27 Th	27 Sa	27 Tu
28 Sa	28 Tu	28 Tu	28 Fr	28 Su	28 We
29 Su		29 We	29 Sa	29 Mo Spring Bank Holiday 22	29 Th
30 Mo 5		30 Th	30 Su	30 Tu	30 Fr
31 Tu		31 Fr		31 We	

July	August	September	October	November	December
1 Sa	1 Tu	1 Fr	1 Su	1 We	1 Fr
2 Su	2 We	2 Sa	2 Mo 40	2 Th	2 Sa
3 Mo 27	3 Th	3 Su	3 Tu	3 Fr	3 Su
4 Tu	4 Fr	4 Mo 36	4 We	4 Sa	4 Mo 49
5 We	5 Sa	5 Tu	5 Th	5 Su	5 Tu
6 Th	6 Su	6 We	6 Fr	6 Mo 45	6 We
7 Fr	7 Mo 32	7 Th	7 Sa	7 Tu	7 Th
8 Sa	8 Tu	8 Fr	8 Su	8 We	8 Fr
9 Su	9 We	9 Sa	9 Mo 41	9 Th	9 Sa
10 Mo 28	10 Th	10 Su	10 Tu	10 Fr	10 Su
11 Tu	11 Fr	11 Mo 37	11 We	11 Sa	11 Mo 50
12 We	12 Sa	12 Tu	12 Th	12 Su	12 Tu
13 Th	13 Su	13 We	13 Fr	13 Mo 46	13 We
14 Fr	14 Mo 33	14 Th	14 Sa	14 Tu	14 Th
15 Sa	15 Tu	15 Fr	15 Su	15 We	15 Fr
16 Su	16 We	16 Sa	16 Mo 42	16 Th	16 Sa
17 Mo 29	17 Th	17 Su	17 Tu	17 Fr	17 Su
18 Tu	18 Fr	18 Mo 38	18 We	18 Sa	18 Mo 51
19 We	19 Sa	19 Tu	19 Th	19 Su	19 Tu
20 Th	20 Su	20 We	20 Fr	20 Mo 47	20 We
21 Fr	21 Mo 34	21 Th	21 Sa	21 Tu	21 Th
22 Sa	22 Tu	22 Fr	22 Su	22 We	22 Fr
23 Su	23 We	23 Sa	23 Mo 43	23 Th	23 Sa
24 Mo 30	24 Th	24 Su	24 Tu	24 Fr	24 Su
25 Tu	25 Fr	25 Mo 39	25 We	25 Sa	25 Mo Christmas Day 52
26 We	26 Sa	26 Tu	26 Th	26 Su	26 Tu Boxing Day
27 Th	27 Su	27 We	27 Fr	27 Mo 48	27 We
28 Fr	28 Mo August Bank Hol. 35	28 Th	28 Sa	28 Tu	28 Th
29 Sa	29 Tu	29 Fr	29 Su	29 We	29 Fr
30 Su	30 We	30 Sa	30 Mo 44	30 Th	30 Sa
31 Mo 31	31 Th		31 Tu		31 Su

5000 WEEKS

LIFE IS TOO SHORT TO BE ANYTHING LESS THAN **HAPPY**

SO **LAUGH** OFTEN,
FORGIVE QUICK,
TAKE **CHANCES**
AND NEVER HAVE **REGRETS**

Activity based goals	Achieved?	Reward planned? – Have FUN!!!

CHUNKING it down... Break down my big "HUGS" for the year into these smaller ACTIVITY based goals for this month.

Monday 26th December 2016

Tuesday 27th December 2016

Wednesday 28th December 2016

Thursday 29th December 2016

Friday 30th December 2016

Saturday 31st December 2016

NEW YEARS EVE!!!

Sunday 1st January 2017
HAPPY NEW YEAR!

Monday 2nd January 2017

Tuesday 3rd January 2017

Wednesday 4th January 2017

Thursday 5th January 2017

Friday 6th January 2017

Saturday 7th January 2017

Sunday 8th January 2017

Monday 9th January 2017

Tuesday 10th January 2017

Wednesday 11th January 2017

Thursday 12th January 2017

Friday 13th January 2017

Saturday 14th January 2017

Sunday 15th January 2017

Monday 16th January 2017

Tuesday 17th January 2017

Wednesday 18th January 2017

Thursday 19th January 2017

Friday 20th January 2017

Saturday 21st January 2017

Sunday 22nd January 2017

Monday 23rd January 2017

Tuesday 24th January 2017

Wednesday 25th January 2017

Thursday 26th January 2017

Friday 27th January 2017

Saturday 28th January 2017

Sunday 29th January 2017

JANUARYS BEST BITS

Write it, draw it or stick it...
Keep a track of your favourite
moments from this month

What did I learn? What am I
proud of?. How did I celebrate?

DO SOMETHING

TODAY

THAT YOUR FUTURE
SELF

WILL

THANK YOU FOR

thank
YOU
SELF from
the past

FEBRUARY 2017

Activity based goals	Achieved?	Reward planned? – Have FUN!!!

CHUNKING it down... Break down my big "HUGS" for the year into these smaller ACTIVITY based goals for this month.

Monday 30th January 2017

Tuesday 31st January 2017

Wednesday 1st February 2017

Thursday 2nd February 2017

Friday 3rd February 2017

Saturday 4th February 2017

Sunday 5th February 2017

Monday 6th February 2017

Tuesday 7th February 2017

Wednesday 8th February 2017

Thursday 9th February 2017

Friday 10th February 2017

Saturday 11th February 2017

Sunday 12th February 2017

Monday 6th February 2017

Monday 13th February 2017

Tuesday 14th February 2017

Happy Valentine's Day

Wednesday 15th February 2017

Thursday 16th February 2017

Friday 17th February 2017

Saturday 18th February 2017

Sunday 19th February 2017

Monday 20th February 2017

Tuesday 21st February 2017

Wednesday 22nd February 2017

Thursday 23rd February 2017

Friday 24th February 2017

Saturday 25th February 2017

Sunday 26th February 2017

THE KEY TO SUCCESS

IS UNDERNEATH YOUR ALARMCLOCK

GET UP JUST 30 MINS
EARLIER AND...
READ, WRITE, WATCH, LEARN,
DO, CREATE, GROW ...

FEBRUARYS BEST BITS

Write it, draw it or stick it...
Keep a track of your favourite
moments from this month

What did I learn? What am I
proud of? How did I celebrate?

Business Dashboards - Let's review my numbers so far in 2017

[Coaches Tip] If you don't know any of these numbers then sit down with your accountant or bookkeeper and ask them to help you. They will help you to set some great goals and objectives for 2017.

It's pointless trying to improve something if you can't measure it.

These are my numbers since Jan 1st 2017

My Turnover since Jan 1st How much I have generated so far this year	
My NET Profit since Jan 1st How much I have made so far this year after all my fixed and variable costs are deducted.	
My Breakeven The amount I currently need to run my business & before I make a profit.	
My Conversion rate (As a percentage) How many leads I need to see before I make a sale represented as a percentage	
My NET Profit Margin (As a percentage) How much money I made after fixed and variable costs are subtracted.	
My repeat business as an average How often my customers come back to me and give me repeat business as an average.	
My Average order value The average order value for all my sales. Total sales value divided by the number of sales.	

MY NUMBERS

I need to focus on the following numbers

Things I can DO to make these numbers better

MARCH 2017

Activity based goals	Achieved?	Reward planned? – Have FUN!!!

CHUNKING it down... Break down my big "HUGS" for the year into these smaller ACTIVITY based goals for this month.

Monday 27th February 2017

Tuesday 28th February 2017

Wednesday 1st March 2017

Thursday 2nd March 2017

Friday 3rd March 2017

Saturday 4th March 2017

Sunday 5th March 2017

Monday 27th February 2017

Monday 6th March 2017

Tuesday 7th March 2017

Wednesday 8th March 2017

Thursday 9th March 2017

Friday 10th March 2017

Saturday 11th March 2017

Sunday 12th March 2017

Monday 13th March 2017

Tuesday 14th March 2017

Wednesday 15th March 2017

Thursday 16th March 2017

Friday 17th March 2017

Saturday 18th March 2017

Sunday 19th March 2017

Monday 13th March 2017

Monday 20th March 2017

Tuesday 21st March 2017

Wednesday 22nd March 2017

Thursday 23rd March 2017

Friday 24th March 2017

Saturday 25th March 2017

Sunday 26th March 2017

Monday 27th March 2017

Tuesday 28th March 2017

Wednesday 29th March 2017

Thursday 30th March 2017

Friday 31st March 2017

Saturday 1st April 2017

APRIL FOOLS DAY!!

Sunday 2nd April 2017

THE TRUE **COST** LIFE OF ANYTHING IN IS THE AMOUNT **TIME** OF YOU ARE WILLING TO **EXCHANGE** FOR IT ...

MARCHS BEST BITS

Write it, draw it or stick it...
Keep a track of your favourite
moments from this month

What did I learn? What am I
proud of? How did I celebrate?

90 DAY CHECK IN

Now is a good time to check-in on my HUG's! How am I doing against my big goals for 2017 — Do I need to adjust my goals or my behaviour to stay on track?

I must keep my HUGS meaningful, relevant and achievable.

Reminder of my HUG — Goal	Notes — How am I doing?
1.	
2.	
3.	
4.	
5.	

List of my original goals goes here.

Am I on-track? — do I need to adjust my actions? — Or do I need to change the goal!?

APRIL 2017

Activity based goals	Achieved?	Reward planned? – Have FUN!!!

CHUNKING it down... Break down my big "HUGS" for the year into these smaller ACTIVITY based goals for this month.

Monday 3rd April 2017

Tuesday 4th April 2017

Wednesday 5th April 2017

Thursday 6th April 2017

Friday 7th April 2017

Saturday 8th April 2017

Sunday 9th April 2017

Monday 10th April 2017

Tuesday 11th April 2017

Wednesday 12th April 2017

Thursday 13th April 2017

Friday 14th April 2017 - Good Friday

Saturday 15th April 2017

Sunday 16th April 2017 - EASTER

Monday 10th April 2017

Monday 17th April 2017 – EASTER MONDAY

Tuesday 18th April 2017

Wednesday 19th April 2017

Thursday 20th April 2017

Friday 21st April 2017

Saturday 22nd April 2017

Sunday 23rd April 2017

Monday 17th April 2017 – EASTER MONDAY

Monday 24th April 2017

Tuesday 25th April 2017

Wednesday 26th April 2017

Thursday 27th April 2017

Friday 28th April 2017

Saturday 29th April 2017

Sunday 30th April 2017

Monday 24th April 2017

LIFE
IS
ABOUT
USING
THE
WHOLE
BOX
OF
CRAYONS

APRILS BEST BITS

Write it, draw it or stick it...
Keep a track of your favourite
moments from this month

What did I learn? What am I
proud of?. How did I celebrate?

Business Dashboards - Let's review my numbers so far in 2017

These are my numbers since Jan 1st 2017

My Turnover since Jan 1st How much I have generated so far this year	
My NET Profit since Jan 1st How much I have made so far this year after all my fixed and variable costs are deducted.	
My Breakeven The amount I currently need to run my business & before I make a profit.	
My Conversion rate (As a percentage) How many leads I need to see before I make a sale represented as a percentage	
My NET Profit Margin (As a percentage) How much money I made after fixed and variable costs are subtracted.	
My repeat business as an average How often my customers come back to me and give me repeat business as an average.	
My Average order value The average order value for all my sales. Total sales value divided by the number of sales.	

MY NUMBERS

I need to focus on the following numbers

Things I can DO to make these numbers better

MAY 2017

Activity based goals	Achieved?	Reward planned? – Have FUN!!!

CHUNKING it down... Break down my big "HUGS" for the year into these smaller ACTIVITY based goals for this month.

Monday 1st May 2017 — (UK) Bank Holiday

Tuesday 2nd May 2017

Wednesday 3rd May 2017

Thursday 4th May 2017

Friday 5th May 2017

Saturday 6th May 2017

Sunday 7th May 2017

Monday 8th May 2017

Tuesday 9th May 2017

Wednesday 10th May 2017

Thursday 11th May 2017

Friday 12th May 2017

Saturday 13th May 2017

Sunday 14th May 2017

Monday 15th May 2017

Tuesday 16th May 2017

Wednesday 17th May 2017

Thursday 18th May 2017

Friday 19th May 2017

Saturday 20th May 2017

Sunday 21st May 2017

Monday 22nd May 2017

Tuesday 23rd May 2017

Wednesday 24th May 2017

Thursday 25th May 2017

Friday 26th May 2017

Saturday 27th May 2017

Sunday 28th May 2017

MAYS BEST BITS

Write it, draw it or stick it...
Keep a track of your favourite
moments from this month

What did I learn? What am I
proud of? How did I celebrate?

YOU WILL NEVER PLOUGH A FIELD

BY TURNING IT OVER IN YOUR MIND

TAKE ACTION !

JUNE 2017

Activity based goals	Achieved?	Reward planned? – Have FUN!!!

CHUNKING it down… Break down my big "HUGS" for the year into these smaller ACTIVITY based goals for this month.

Monday 29th May 2017 — (UK) Bank Holiday

Tuesday 30th May 2017

Wednesday 31st May 2017

Thursday 1st June 2017

Friday 2nd June 2017

Saturday 3rd June 2017

Sunday 4th June 2017

Monday 5th June 2017

Tuesday 6th June 2017

Wednesday 7th June 2017

Thursday 8th June 2017

Friday 9th June 2017

Saturday 10th June 2017

Sunday 11th June 2017

Monday 5th June 2017

Monday 12th June 2017

Tuesday 13th June 2017

Wednesday 14th June 2017

Thursday 15th June 2017

Friday 16th June 2017

Saturday 17th June 2017

Sunday 18th June 2017

Monday 19th June 2017

Tuesday 20th June 2017

Wednesday 21st June 2017

Thursday 22nd June 2017

Friday 23rd June 2017

Saturday 24th June 2017

Sunday 25th June 2017

Monday 19th June 2017

Monday 26th June 2017

Tuesday 27th June 2017

Wednesday 28th June 2017

Thursday 29th June 2017

Friday 30th June 2017

Saturday 1st July 2017

Sunday 2nd July 2017

JUNES BEST BITS

Write it, draw it or stick it...
Keep a track of my favourite
moments from this month

What did I learn? What am I proud
of? How did I celebrate?

When you FEEL LIKE QUITTING think about WHY YOU STARTED

90 DAY CHECK IN

Now is a good time to check-in on my HUG's! How am I doing against my BIG goals for 2017 – Do I need to adjust my goals or my behaviour to stay on track?

I must keep my HUGS meaningful, relevant and achievable.

Reminder of my HUG – Goal	Notes- How am I doing?
1.	
2.	
3.	
4.	
5.	

List of my original goals goes here.

Am I on-track? – do I need to adjust my actions? – Or do I need to change the goal!?

JULY 2017

Activity based goals	Achieved?	Reward planned? – Have FUN!!!

CHUNKING it down... Break down my big "HUGS" for the year into these smaller ACTIVITY based goals for this month.

Monday 3rd July 2017

Tuesday 4th July 2017

Wednesday 5th July 2017

Thursday 6th July 2017

Friday 7th July 2017

Saturday 8th July 2017

Sunday 9th July 2017

Monday 3rd July 2017

Monday 10th July 2017

Tuesday 11th July 2017

Wednesday 12th July 2017

Thursday 13th July 2017

Friday 14th July 2017

Saturday 15th July 2017

Sunday 16th July 2017

Monday 17th July 2017

Tuesday 18th July 2017

Wednesday 19th July 2017

Thursday 20th July 2017

Friday 21st July 2017

Saturday 22nd July 2017

Sunday 23rd July 2017

Monday 17th July 2017

Monday 24th July 2017

Tuesday 25th July 2017

Wednesday 26th July 2017

Thursday 27th July 2017

Friday 28th July 2017

Saturday 29th July 2017

Sunday 30th July 2017

Monday 24th July 2017

JULYS BEST BITS

Write it, draw it or stick it...
Keep a track of my favourite
moments from this month

What did I learn? What am I
proud of? How did I celebrate?

THIS MONTH

LESS

MORE

LESS	MORE
THINKING	DOING
FROWNING	SMILING
TALKING	LISTENING
JUDGING	ACCEPTING
WATCHING	READING
COMPLAINING	BELIEVING
DOUBTING	APPRECIATING
DREAMING	CREATING

LESS

MORE

Business Dashboards - Let's review my numbers so far in 2017

[Coaches Tip] If you don't know any of these numbers then sit down with your accountant or bookkeeper and ask them to help you. They will help you to set some great goals and objectives for 2017.

It's pointless trying to improve something if you can't measure it.

These are my numbers since Jan 1st 2017

My Turnover since Jan 1st How much I have generated so far this year	
My NET Profit since Jan 1st How much I have made so far this year after all my fixed and variable costs are deducted.	
My Breakeven The amount I currently need to run my business & before I make a profit.	
My Conversion rate (As a percentage) How many leads I need to see before I make a sale represented as a percentage	
My NET Profit Margin (As a percentage) How much money I made after fixed and variable costs are subtracted.	
My repeat business as an average How often my customers come back to me and give me repeat business as an average.	
My Average order value The average order value for all my sales. Total sales value divided by the number of sales.	

MY NUMBERS

I need to focus on the following numbers

Things I can DO to make these numbers better

AUGUST 2017

Activity based goals	Achieved?	Reward planned? – Have FUN!!!

CHUNKING it down... Break down my big "HUGS" for the year into these smaller ACTIVITY based goals for this month.

Monday 31st July 2017

Tuesday 1st August 2017

Wednesday 2nd August 2017

Thursday 3rd August 2017

Friday 4th August 2017

Saturday 5th August 2017

Sunday 6th August 2017

Monday 31st July 2017

Monday 7th August 2017

Tuesday 8th August 2017

Wednesday 9th August 2017

Thursday 10th August 2017

Friday 11th August 2017

Saturday 12th August 2017

Sunday 13th August 2017

Monday 14th August 2017

Tuesday 15th August 2017

Wednesday 16th August 2017

Thursday 17th August 2017

Friday 18th August 2017

Saturday 19th August 2017

Sunday 20th August 2017

Monday 21st August 2017

Tuesday 22nd August 2017

Wednesday 23rd August 2017

Thursday 24th August 2017

Friday 25th August 2017

Saturday 26th August 2017

Sunday 27th August 2017

AUGUSTS BEST BITS

Write it, draw it or stick it...
Keep a track of my favourite moments from this month

What did I learn? What am I proud of? How did I celebrate?

SEPTEMBER 2017

Activity based goals	Achieved?	Reward planned? – Have FUN!!!

CHUNKING it down... Break down my big "HUGS" for the year into these smaller ACTIVITY based goals for this month.

Monday 28th August 2017 – (UK) Bank Holiday

Tuesday 29th August 2017

Wednesday 30th August 2017

Thursday 31st August 2017

Friday 1st September 2017

Saturday 2nd September 2017

Sunday 3rd September 2017

Monday 4th September 2017

Tuesday 5th September 2017

Wednesday 6th September 2017

Thursday 7th September 2017

Friday 8th September 2017

Saturday 9th September 2017

Sunday 10th September 2017

Monday 11th September 2017

Tuesday 12th September 2017

Wednesday 13th September 2017

Thursday 14th September 2017

Friday 15th September 2017

Saturday 16th September 2017

Sunday 17th September 2017

Monday 11th September 2017

Monday 18th September 2017

Tuesday 19th September 2017

Wednesday 20th September 2017

Thursday 21st September 2017

Friday 22nd September 2017

Saturday 23rd September 2017

Sunday 24th September 2017

Monday 25th September 2017

Tuesday 26th September 2017

Wednesday 27th September 2017

Thursday 28th September 2017

Friday 29th September 2017

Saturday 30th September 2017

Sunday 1st October 2017

SEPTEMBERS BEST BITS

Write it, draw it or stick it...
Keep a track of my favourite
moments from this month

What did I learn? What am I
proud of?. How did I celebrate?

90 DAY CHECK IN

Now is a good time to check-in on my HUG's! How am I doing against my BIG goals for 2017 — Do I need to adjust my goals or my behaviour to stay on track?

I must keep my HUGS meaningful, relevant and achievable.

Reminder of my HUG – Goal	Notes – How am I doing?
1.	
2.	
3.	
4.	
5.	

List of my original goals goes here.

Am I on-track? — do I need to adjust my actions? — Or do I need to change the goal!?

OCTOBER 2017

Activity based goals	Achieved?	Reward planned? – Have FUN!!!

CHUNKING it down... Break down my big "HUGS" for the year into these smaller ACTIVITY based goals for this month.

Monday 2ⁿᵈ October 2017

Tuesday 3ʳᵈ October 2017

Wednesday 4ᵗʰ October 2017

Thursday 5ᵗʰ October 2017

Friday 6ᵗʰ October 2017

Saturday 7ᵗʰ October 2017

Sunday 8ᵗʰ October 2017

Monday 2ⁿᵈ October 2017

Monday 9th October 2017

Tuesday 10th October 2017

Wednesday 11th October 2017

Thursday 12th October 2017

Friday 13th October 2017

Saturday 14th October 2017

Sunday 15th October 2017

Monday 9th October 2017

Monday 16th October 2017

Tuesday 17th October 2017

Wednesday 18th October 2017

Thursday 19th October 2017

Friday 20th October 2017

Saturday 21st October 2017

Sunday 22nd October 2017

Monday 23rd October 2017

Tuesday 24th October 2017

Wednesday 25th October 2017

Thursday 26th October 2017

Friday 27th October 2017

Saturday 28th October 2017

Sunday 29th October 2017

OCTOBERS BEST BITS

Write it, draw it or stick it...
Keep a track of my favourite
moments from this month

What did I learn? What am I
proud of?. How did I celebrate?

Business Dashboards - Let's review my numbers so far in 2017

[Coaches Tip] If you don't know any of these numbers then sit down with your accountant or bookkeeper and ask them to help you. They will help you to set some great goals and objectives for 2017.

It's pointless trying to improve something if you can't measure it.

These are my numbers since Jan 1st 2017

My Turnover since Jan 1st How much I have generated so far this year	
My NET Profit since Jan 1st How much I have made so far this year after all my fixed and variable costs are deducted.	
My Breakeven The amount I currently need to run my business & before I make a profit.	
My Conversion rate (As a percentage) How many leads I need to see before I make a sale represented as a percentage	
My NET Profit Margin (As a percentage) How much money I made after fixed and variable costs are subtracted.	
My repeat business as an average How often my customers come back to me and give me repeat business as an average.	
My Average order value The average order value for all my sales. Total sales value divided by the number of sales.	

MY NUMBERS

I need to focus on the following numbers

Things I can DO to make these numbers better

NOVEMBER 2017

Activity based goals	Achieved?	Reward planned? – Have FUN!!!
REMEMBER TO ORDER MY 2018 DIARY!!!!!		

CHUNKING it down... Break down my big "HUGS" for the year into these smaller ACTIVITY based goals for this month.

Monday 30th October 2017

Tuesday 31st October 2017

Wednesday 1st November 2017

Thursday 2nd November 2017

Friday 3rd November 2017

Saturday 4th November 2017

Sunday 5th November 2017

Monday 6th November 2017

Tuesday 7th November 2017

Wednesday 8th November 2017

Thursday 9th November 2017

Friday 10th November 2017

Saturday 11th November 2017

Sunday 12th November 2017

Monday 13th November 2017

Tuesday 14th November 2017

Wednesday 15th November 2017

Thursday 16th November 2017

Friday 17th November 2017

Saturday 18th November 2017

Sunday 19th November 2017

Monday 20th November 2017

Tuesday 21st November 2017

Wednesday 22nd November 2017

Thursday 23rd November 2017

Friday 24th November 2017

Saturday 25th November 2017

Sunday 26th November 2017

NOVEMBERS BEST BITS

Write it, draw it or stick it...
Keep a track of my favourite
moments from this month

What did I learn? What am I
proud of? How did I celebrate?

IF YOU DON'T CLIMB YOU CAN'T FALL

BUT THERE IS
NO FUN IN

SPENDING
YOUR WHOLE
LIFE ON
THE GROUND!

DECEMBER 2017

Activity based goals	Achieved?	Reward planned? – Have FUN!!!

CHUNKING it down... Break down my big "HUGS" for the year into these smaller ACTIVITY based goals for this month.

Monday 27th November 2017

Tuesday 28th November 2017

Wednesday 29th November 2017

Thursday 30th November 2017

Friday 1st December 2017

Saturday 2nd December 2017

Sunday 3rd December 2017

Monday 4th December 2017

Tuesday 5th December 2017

Wednesday 6th December 2017

Thursday 7th December 2017

Friday 8th December 2017

Saturday 9th December 2017

Sunday 10th December 2017

Monday 4th December 2017

Monday 11th December 2017

Tuesday 12th December 2017

Wednesday 13th December 2017

Thursday 14th December 2017

Friday 15th December 2017

Saturday 16th December 2017

Sunday 17th December 2017

Monday 11th December 2017

Monday 18th December 2017

Tuesday 19th December 2017

Wednesday 20th December 2017

Thursday 21st December 2017

Friday 22nd December 2017

Saturday 23rd December 2017

Sunday 24th December 2017
Christmas Eve

Monday 25th December 2017 – Christmas Day

Tuesday 26th December 2017 – Boxing Day

Wednesday 27th December 2017

Thursday 28th December 2017

Friday 29th December 2017

Saturday 30th December 2017

Sunday 31st December 2017
New Year's Eve

Monday 1st January 2018 – Happy New Year!

Tuesday 2nd January 2018

Wednesday 3rd January 2018

Thursday 4th January 2018

Friday 4th January 2018

Saturday 6th January 2018

Sunday 7th January 2018

Monday 1st January 2018 – Happy New Year!

DECEMBERS BEST BITS

Write it, draw it or stick it...
Keep a track of my favourite
moments from this month

What did I learn? What am I
proud of? How did I celebrate?

HUG – Goal	How did I do?????
[Example] To increase my revenue by at least 20%	I SMASHED it by 30%
1.	
2.	
3.	
4.	
5.	

TIME TO REFLECT

What I LOVED about 2017

What I'd CHANGE about 2017

MY NOTES

www.ingramcontent.com/pod-product-compliance
Lightning Source LLC
Chambersburg PA
CBHW081154180526
45170CB00006B/2076